GW00708407

ECDL PART 2

BCS Level 2 Certificate for IT Users
Unit E – Using IT

O.H.U. Heathcote

Published by

PAYNE-GALLWAY
P U B L I S H E R S   L T D

26-28 Northgate Street, Ipswich IP1 3DB
Tel: 01473 251097 Fax: 01473 232758

www.payne-gallway.co.uk

Acknowledgements

Cover design by direction123.com

First Edition 2004

A catalogue entry for this book is available from the British Library.

ISBN 1 904467 48 2

Copyright © O. H. U. Heathcote 2004

The ECDL Trade Mark is the registered trade mark of The European Computer Driving Licence Foundation Limited in Ireland and other countries.

The BCS Trade Mark is the registered trade mark of the British Computer Society.

This ECDL courseware product incorporates learning reinforcement exercises. These exercises are included to help the candidate in their training for the ECDL Part 2. The exercises included in this courseware product are not BCS certification tests and should not be construed in any way as BCS certification tests. For information about Authorised BCS Test Centres please refer to the BCS web site at www.bcs.org

All rights reserved

No part of this publication may be reproduced, stored in a retrieval system, or transmitted in any form or by any means, electronic, mechanical, photocopying, recording, or otherwise, without the prior permission of the copyright owners.

The authors and publisher shall not be liable for any damage caused or alleged to be caused either directly or indirectly, by this book.

All data presented in this book is entirely fictional.

Printed in the UK by Cromwell Press.

Preface

Who is this book for?

This book is suitable for anyone studying Unit E of the BCS Level 2 Certificate for IT Users (ECDL Part 2), either at school, adult class or at home. It is suitable for those who have completed ECDL modules 1-7 and takes the learner step-by-step to the point where they will feel confident using different software applications to handle data.

The approach

The approach is very much one of "learning by doing". The book is divided into a number of chapters which correspond to one lesson. The student is guided step-by-step through a practical task at the computer, with numerous screenshots to show exactly what should be on their screen at each stage. Each individual in a class can proceed at their own pace, with little or no help from a teacher. At the end of most chapters there are exercises which provide invaluable practice. By the time a student has completed the book, every aspect of the Unit E syllabus will have been covered.

Software used

The instructions and screenshots are based on a PC running Microsoft Windows XP and Microsoft Office 2003. However, it will be relatively easy to adapt the instructions for use with other versions of Windows and Office.

Extra resources

Answers to practice exercises, a cross-reference showing on which page every topic in the ECDL Part 2 Unit E is covered and other useful supporting material can be found on the publisher's web site www.payne-gallway.co.uk/ecdl.

About ECDL

The European Computer Driving Licence (ECDL) is the European-wide qualification enabling people to demonstrate their competence in computer skills. Candidates must study and pass the test for each of the seven modules listed below before they are awarded an ECDL certificate. The ECDL tests must be undertaken at an accredited test centre. For more details of ECDL tests and test centres, visit the ECDL web site www.ecdl.com.

Module 1: Concepts of Information Technology

Module 2: Using the Computer and Managing Files

Module 3: Word Processing

Module 4: Spreadsheets

Module 5: Database

Module 6: Presentation

Module 7: Information and Communication

About the BCS Certificate for IT Users

The level 1 certificate (ECDL Part 1) is made up of 3 units corresponding to ECDL modules 1, 2 and 7.

The level 2 certificate (ECDL Part 2) is made up of 5 units corresponding to ECDL modules 3, 4, 5, 6 and an additional module, Unit E.

This unit is assessed by the BCS. For further details visit the BCS web site www.bcs.org.

ECDL Part 2

Unit E – Using IT

This module requires you to demonstrate knowledge and understanding of a series of theoretical elements such as legal issues associated with computing, health and safety, and good practice. Additionally you will demonstrate your understanding of integration between computer applications and the relevance of each to everyday tasks. You will learn how to:

- Import data
- Transfer it between applications
- Protect it and people affected by it

Table of Contents

Introduction

In the preceding ECDL modules 1-7 you will have seen how to use each of the application programs in detail to produce a document, a spreadsheet, a database, and so on. This book aims to integrate several of these so as to give an overall view of how an organisation might use the data it collects, and how legal restraints affect what it does with it.

Databases, spreadsheets and word processors are all applications that are specialised at doing different things, although there is some overlap between them.

Why use different applications?

Why use **Access**? You can store large amounts of data safely in related tables, analyse it and make reports.

Why use **Excel**? It is very good for doing calculations and showing in an instant the effect of changing a value. You can also draw a graph or chart to show information in a form that is easy to grasp.

Why use **Word**? You can produce polished documents (or even books) and incorporate charts from Excel, or use data from Excel or Access in a mail merge.

It is often necessary to use all three applications to process data but switching between them is not difficult. Other common applications that we shall not deal with here are:

PowerPoint	for presentations
Publisher	for desktop publishing
Outlook	for e-mail, contacts and appointments
FrontPage	for web page creation
Internet Explorer	for browsing web pages

The scenario

In this book we consider an Internet holiday company which saves data from people filling in booking forms on the Internet to take different tours. This is a normal thing for an organisation to do so that they can use it to:

❶   make decisions on what changes to make to their programme

ⓘ   keep their customers up-to-date with regular mailings

ⓘ   analyse their financial data and use it to ensure they stay profitable

The information the company is interested in is the name, address, gender and age range of the person booking, number in the group, type and cost of the holiday, and the booking date. The data is held as a text file.

The data fields are:

Field Names	Description
Title	Mr, Mrs, Ms, Dr, Rev etc.
Initials	
Surname	
Address1	
Address2	
Town	
County	
Postcode	
Tel	Phone number
Gender	M or F
AgeRange	1-4: (18-29; 30-45; 46-60; over 60)
HolType	Holiday type 1-3: (Activity, Beach, Cruise)
Cost	Price per person in group
Group	No. of people booked
Date	Date of holiday
FirstTime	First holiday with this company

The data is held on the web site as a text file, with field names, and needs to be downloaded to a given folder.

Downloading the data

▶   Open your web browser, go to www.payne-gallway.co.uk/ecdl and click on **Student Resources** at the bottom.

▶   Click on **Unit E** and choose **Save Target As** to download the file **Bookings.txt**.

Word prepares to save the **file**.

▶   Click on the **My Documents** button on the left side, then on the **New Folder** button and make a new folder **ECDL8**.

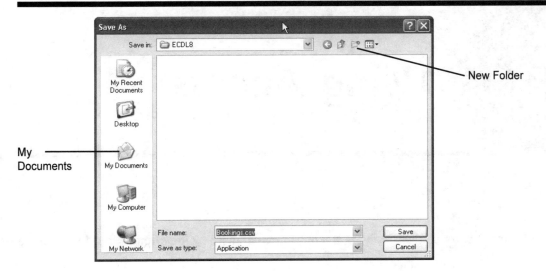

○ Click **Save** to download the file. This will take only a few seconds.

○ Click **Start, My Documents** to open Windows Explorer.

○ On the **View** menu click **Details**.

○ Click the **Folders** button and select the **ECDL8** folder.

You can now see the imported file in its folder in Windows Explorer.

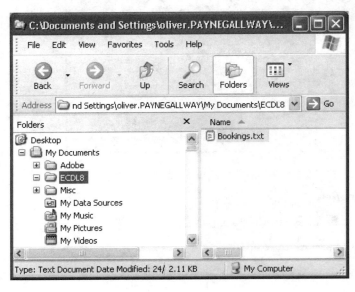

CHAPTER 2

Using Access

In this chapter you will transfer the data to a database by **importing** it into Microsoft Access.

Opening Access

● *Either* double-click the **Access** icon on the Windows desktop

● *Or* select **Start** then **Programs** then

You will see a screen like the following:

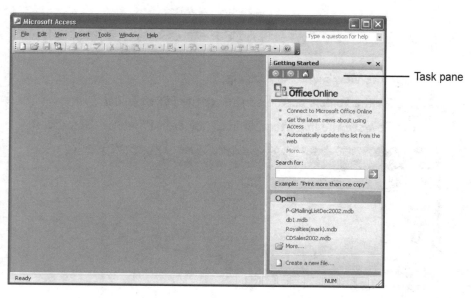

First you need to create a new database to hold the data.

● Select **File, New**.

● Click **Blank Database** in the Task pane.

The File New Database window opens.

● In the **Save in** box, navigate to your **ECDL8** folder.

○ In the **File name** box change the name to **Bookings.mdb** and click **Create**.

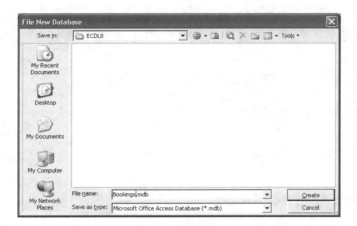

The database window opens for the **Bookings** database. Note that it has no tables yet.

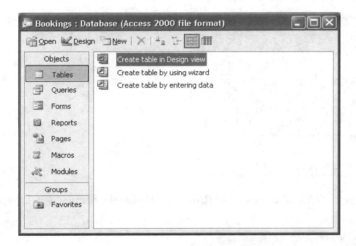

Importing data

Time to bring in the data! Here we could create the table and its fields first but it's easier to get Access to set up the table for us from the data imported.

○ Choose **File, Get External Data, Import**.

In the Import window, the **Look in** box should be set to the **ECDL8** folder.

○ In the **Files of type** list, scroll down to **Text files (*.txt, *.csv, *.tab, *.asc)**.

This should reveal your downloaded file **Bookings.txt** – if not you will need to have a look for it in adjacent folders.

○ Select **Bookings.txt** and click the **Import** button.

The **Import Text Wizard** analyses the data and needs to know whether the fields are of fixed width, or separated (**delimited**) by commas or tabs.

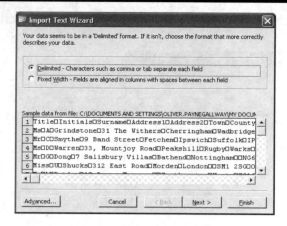

> ⊙ Leave **Delimited** and click **Next**.

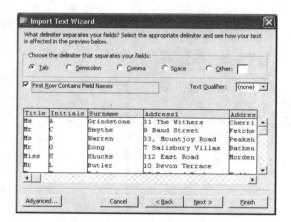

> ⊙ Leave **Tab** selected and check **First Row Contains Field Names**. Click **Next**.

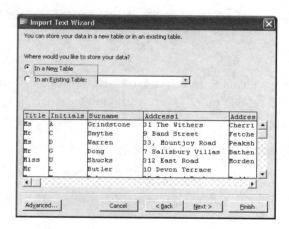

> ⊙ Leave **In a New Table** selected and click **Next**.

At this point you could set all the data types (but this is easier to do later), and skip any fields you didn't want to import.

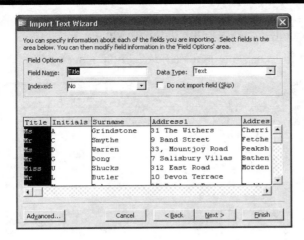

○   Click **Next**.

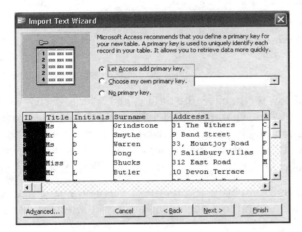

○   Select **Let Access add primary key** and notice a new **ID** field appears. Click **Next**.

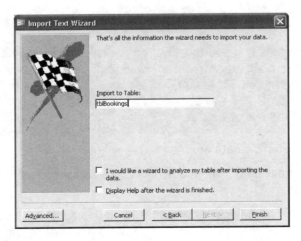

○   Under **Import to Table** enter **tblBookings** and click **Finish**.

The wizard now imports the data – this may take a minute or two – and tells you when this is complete. The new table appears in the database window.

Open ──○ Click the **Open** button to see the imported data in datasheet view.

	ID	Title	Initials	Surname	Address1	Address2	Town	County	Postcode	Tel
►	1	Ms	A	Grindstone	31 The Withers	Cherringham	Wadbridge	Suffolk	IP21 4KB	01394 450
	2	Mr	C	Smythe	9 Band Street	Fetchem	Ipswich	Suffolk	IP8 4GF	01473 350
	3	Ms	D	Warren	33, Mountjoy R	Peakshill	Rugby	Warks	CV21 3QS	01788 284
	4	Mr	G	Dong	7 Salisbury Vill:	Bathend	Nottingham		NG6 0NB	0115 925 :
	5	Miss	U	Shucks	312 East Road	Morden	London		SM1 2SG	01929 247
	6	Mr	L	Butler	10 Devon Terrad		Southampton	Hants	SO16 9RJ	023 805 1
	7	Mr	M	Baker	25 Rutland Parl	Madding	Banbury	Oxon	OX16 9QA	01295 893
	8	Mr	A	Haroun	17 Spencer Ro:	Tooting	London		SW17 6GM	0208 458 :
	9	Mr	E	Williams	100 Mancheste		Winchester	Hants	SO22 6RX	01962 766
	10	Mrs	S	Tickle	42 Bath Road		Leeds	W Yorks	LS9 7NL	01943 872
	11	Mr	Z	Kevan	11 Milland Roac	Gotham	Liverpool		L7 9SJ	0151 383 ,
	12	Mrs	V	Wilkinson	45 Bank End L:		Wolverhampton	W Midlands	SA9 1AP	01902 836
	13	Dr	N	Wade	12 Old Bedford		Runcorn	Cheshire	WA7 4SY	01928 867
	14	Miss	H	Williams	18 Peakshill Ri:		Chippenham	Wilts	SN15 3QD	01249 459

Record: 14 ◄ 1 ► ►I ►* of 24

You can scroll down to see the data neatly slotted into the correct fields. Was that quicker than typing it in?

○ Close the datasheet window.

Formats for transferring data

When importing data into, say, a database, the data is just a long stream of characters so it is essential to indicate what separates different fields and what indicates the end of a record. If this is not done, the importing software will not know how to chop the data up and may end up putting it all in one record or even in one field! Where a table is already defined, the imported data must slot exactly into the database 'framework'.

For a database, data is normally imported as plain text, since stray characters – for example those indicating formatting in a document file – will interfere. The most common formats are:

❶ **Comma-delimited** – usually **.csv** for **comma-separated values**

❶ **Tab-delimited** – usually **.txt** but can be **.asc** or **.tab**

Caution:

The limitation of .csv format is that you **must not** have a comma in any field unless the field text is in quotes, otherwise it will be interpreted as the start of the next field. An address entered as **33, Mountjoy Road** as in the third record shown above will then occupy 2 fields not 1, with everything in that record after 33 going into the wrong field. Tab-delimited is safer.

Other formats used for transferring data are:

❶ **Data Interchange Format (.dif)** – originally between spreadsheets and databases but now seldom used.

❶ **Rich Text Format (.rtf)** saves document formatting and images; it is used to transfer data between quite different word processors or e-mail, although some formatting may be lost.

Setting the field data types

Access holds different types of data as specific data types. These are:

Text	Letters, symbols and numbers, i.e. **Alphanumeric** data.
Number	Numbers only (no letters). Includes numbers with decimal points.
Date/Time	Dates and times.
Currency	For monetary data. Access inserts a currency symbol in front eg £
Yes/No	For where the field can be one of only 2 values, Y/N, True/False.
AutoNumber	A unique value generated by Access for each record.

Some of these types enable Access to do calculations on the data. For example, two dates could be entered as text fields but then Access would not be able to calculate which date was later or how many days apart they were, as calculations cannot be done on a text field.

When Access imports data it makes a guess at a field type if, for example, it looks like a number or date.

   ● In the database window click the **Design** button.

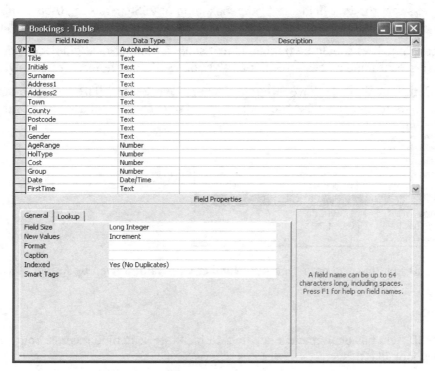

In the table design window, Access has imported the field names and given data types mostly of Text but it has recognised numbers and dates.

● Change the fields as in the following table, entering the data type, field size where relevant, and description.

Field	Data type	Field size	Description
Title	Text	6	
Initials	Text	4	
Surname	Text	30	
Address1	Text	30	
Address2	Text	30	
Town	Text	30	
County	Text	30	
Postcode	Text	10	
Tel	Text	20	Contact number
Gender	Text	1	M / F
AgeRange	Number	Integer	Age range code 1-4
HolType	Number	Integer	Holiday type code 1-3
Cost	Currency		Cost of 1 holiday
Group	Number	Integer	Number of people booked
Date	Date/Time	Short Date	Date of holiday
FirstTime	Yes/No		First booking

Access sets the text field size to the maximum of 255 characters. (Above this the **Memo** type handles larger amounts of text.) All the text field sizes need to be reduced.

Phone numbers should be treated as text since a **Number** field type does not allow spaces or leading zeroes – so that **01473 252866** would be recorded as **1473252866**.

A **Date/Time** field can have different **Formats** from **General Date** including both date and time to long, medium and short versions of each: we will use **Short Date**. Note the **/** delimiter.

General Date	19/06/1994 17:34:23
Long Date	19 June 1994
Medium Date	19-Jun-94
Short Date	19/06/1994
Long Time	17:34:23
Medium Time	05:34 PM
Short Time	17:34

The **ID** field has the data type **AutoNumber** with values given by Access.

The key field

The ID field has been made a key field to facilitate searching records. Your fields should now look like this:

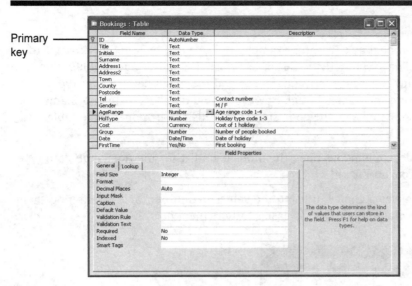

Primary key

Click the **Close** icon to close the window and **Yes** to save.

Note:

Access may give a message that data could be lost by the new field definitions: you can ignore this.

Adding a validation

When data is first entered it is most important that it should be accurate with as few mistakes as possible, and to help with this there can be **validation** checks to catch any entries which are obviously wrong. In the present case there would have been checks on the Internet booking form but it is advisable to check again in case data is entered directly into the database.

Some fields can only hold certain values. The **Yes / No** data type allows only two options such as Yes or No, True or False, and is usually shown as a check box. The **Gender** field could also have been a Yes / No field but is a text field of one character. It needs to accept only values of **M** or **F**.

- Open the Design window again.

- In the Field Properties for **Gender**, click in **Validation Rule** and type **M or F**. Access adds quotes.

- For **Validation Text** type **Gender must be M or F**.

- Save and close the design window. Access will warn you that data could be affected by this: click **OK**.

- Open the table in Datasheet view, change a gender to, say, **X**, and press **Tab** or click in another field.

Access will warn you that this cannot be done. This would also happen if you were to import a record with an invalid gender.

- Click **OK** and click **Undo**.

Lookup codes

Field values are often held as codes, for example, **HolType** can be a number from 1 to 3 representing the holiday type **Activity**, **Beach** or **Cruise**. The advantage of doing this is that the codes occupy less space in the database and there will be far fewer typing mistakes than entering the names in full. However, using numbers instead of names we need to be able to look up what the code stands for. This can be done in the table definition.

Text
Memo
Number
Date/Time
Currency
AutoNumber
Yes/No
OLE Object
Hyperlink
Lookup Wizard..

▶ In the table design window, open the drop-down list for the **AgeRange** data type and choose **Lookup Wizard**.

The Lookup Wizard gives a choice of using the values in another table or entering them manually. Since there are only four it is easier to type them in.

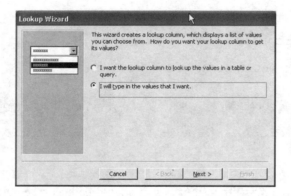

▶ Select **I will type in the values that I want** and click **Next**.

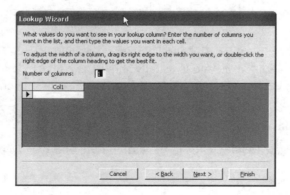

The lookup table needs 2 columns, 1 for the code and 2 for what it stands for.

▶ For **Number of columns** enter **2**.

▶ Enter the values shown on the left. Move to the next row using the down-arrow: don't press Return. (If you do press Return, click **Back**.)

Col1	Col2
1	18-29
2	30-45
3	46-60
4	Over 60
*	

▶ Make the columns narrower by double-clicking between the headings.

▶ Click **Next**.

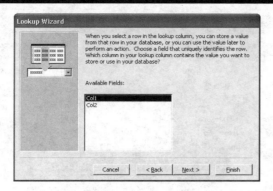

○ Leave **Col1** selected so that the code will be stored in the database. Click **Next** then **Finish**.

○ Notice the lookup parameters in the **Lookup** tab on the Field Properties window.

○ Now for the **HolType** field, set the field size to 1 and make a similar lookup table with the values shown on the left.

○ Save the design window ignoring the warning about lost data, and close it.

○ Open the table in datasheet view and notice the **AgeRange** and **HolType** fields each have a drop-down list showing the code values.

You can change the value either by typing over it or by selecting from the list.

Note:

It is more convenient to enter and view data in a form rather than in datasheet view. Making a form is described in **Pass ECDL4 Module 5**.

Finding data

With a few records, it is easy to look up something but with hundreds of records you need the Find tool.

○ Open **tblBookings** in datasheet view and make the columns narrower by double-clicking or dragging between the column headers.

○ Click anywhere in the **Surname** column then click on the **Find** button.

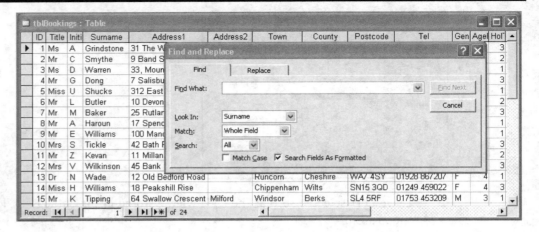

The Find and Replace dialogue looks for text occupying a whole field, the start or any part of it. To find all bookings made by a Williams:

● Type **williams** in the **Find What** box and click **Find Next**.

Access highlights the first occurrence.

● Keep pressing **Find Next** to see all the other bookings by a Williams.

● To see the names beginning with a character, enter **w**, set the **Match** to **Start of Field** and search as before.

Using wildcards

Wildcards are used to represent other characters in a search. An asterisk ***** can stand for any number of characters, while **?** represents a single character and **#** a single number. Entering **wil*son** finds Williamson and Wilkinson, **will*** finds Williams and Williamson and **wil?i** finds all three. Try this yourself.

? is useful for finding different spellings of a word, so that **licen?e** finds both **license** and **licence**. **b??** finds three-letter words starting with **b**.

1#5 finds **105**, **115**, .. and **J7## LD?** might be used for car registrations.

● Close the table, saving the changes.

Of course if the data has been entered carelessly, like **wllaims**, you may not find some records at all! It is essential to be as accurate as possible.

Sorting data

You can sort the data in order of a field by clicking in that column and selecting **Sort Ascending** (or **Sort Descending**).

Querying the data

We can also find all the records that satisfy certain conditions, such as:

- ❶ How many people under age 60 chose a cruise?
- ❶ How many in the lower two age ranges chose a beach holiday?
- ❶ What was the total amount paid during the Summer?

This is done by forming queries. Each query can be saved and used again.

- ◗ In the database window, select the **Queries** tab.

- ◗ Select **Create query in Design view** and click **New**.

- ◗ Leave **Design View** selected and click **OK**.

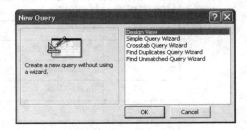

- ◗ with **tblBookings** selected click **Add** then **Close**.

The query design window opens ready for fields to be entered from the table.

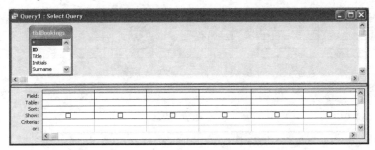

- ◗ In the **tblBookings** list, double-click on each of the fields from **Title** to **Postcode**, **AgeRange**, **HolType** and **Date**. Notice each field is entered in the grid below. Double-click the header between fields to make them narrower.

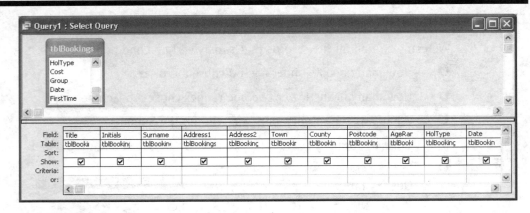

To find out how many non-pensioners chose cruises, we need to know how many in age ranges less than 4 bought holiday type 3.

Comparison operators

This calls for operators which compare a given field with a set value.

Operator	Meaning	Example
<	less than	<20
<=	less than or equal to	<=20
>	greater than	>0
>=	greater than or equal to	>=0
=	equal to	=20
<>	not equal to	<>"Jones"
AND	All criteria must be satisfied	HolType>1 AND Cost<200
OR	At least one of the criteria must be satisfied	="Miss" OR "Ms"
NOT	At least one of the criteria must not be satisfied	NOT "Rev"

● In the **Criteria** row, for **AgeRange** enter **<=3** and for **HolType** enter **=3**

Field:	Title	Initials	Surname	Address1	Address2	Town	County	Postcode	AgeRange	HolType	Date
Table:	tblBooki	tblBookin	tblBookin	tblBookings	tblBookin	tblBookir	tblBookin	tblBookin	tblBookin	tblBookin	tblBookin
Sort:											
Show:	☑	☑	☑	☑	☑	☑	☑	☑	☑	☑	☑
Criteria:									<=3	=3	
or:											

● Save the query, giving it the name **qryCruise**.

● Run the query. Access lists the bookings that match the criteria.

Tip:
The **Sort** row in the query grid allows you to sort the results by many levels. The sort order goes from the left so may need fields to be moved.

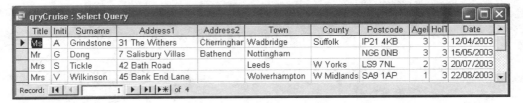

◑   Close the window.

Setting criteria for different fields finds records that match both age range AND holiday type. If we wanted to see those customers that are either travelling alone or for the first time, this needs an OR query between fields as opposed to within a field, for example Title = "Miss" OR "Ms".

◑   In the database window, select the **Queries** tab, click **New, OK**, and add **tblBookings** as before.

◑   Add the fields **Title** to **Surname, Postcode, Group, Date, FirstTime**.

◑   In the **OR** row, enter **=1** under **Group** and **=YES** for **FirstTime**.

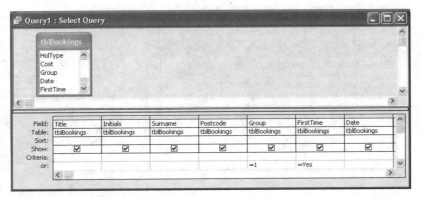

◑   Save the query as **qryAloneFirstTime**.

◑   Run the query to see how many records match.

◑   Close the window.

Using calculated fields in a query

In a database, where you have two values such as quantity ordered of an item and the unit cost, it is not necessary to store the total as well in another field since this can easily be calculated. Suppose we need to know the total value of each booking taken in the second half of 2003? This will be the product of **Cost** and **Group**.

O   Make a new query and add the fields **ID, Surname, Postcode, Cost, Group** and **Date**.

O   In the **Criteria** for **Date**, enter **>30/06/2003 AND <31/12/2003** (widen the column to see it).

Access adds **#** characters around the dates when you leave the box. The calculated field requires a new column.

O   In the **Field** row for the first blank column, enter **[Cost]*[Group]**

As you press **Enter** or tab out of the column, Access adds **Expr1:** as the field name for the calculation.

Field:	ID	Surname	Postcode	Cost	Group	Date	Expr1: [Cost]*[Grou
Table:	tblBookings	tblBookings	tblBookings	tblBookings	tblBookings	tblBookings	
Sort:							
Show:	☑	☑	☑	☑	☑	☑	☑
Criteria:						>#30/06/2003# And <#31/12/2003#	
or:							

O   Save the query as **qryTotal** and run it.

ID	Surname	Postcode	Cost	Gro	Date	Expr1
8	Haroun	SW17 6GM	£240.00	2	07/07/2003	£480.00
9	Williams	SO22 6RX	£266.00	1	19/07/2003	£266.00
10	Tickle	LS9 7NL	£364.00	1	20/07/2003	£364.00
11	Kevan	L7 9SJ	£145.00	2	21/07/2003	£290.00
12	Wilkinson	SA9 1AP	£398.00	3	22/08/2003	£1,194.00
13	Wade	WA7 4SY	£275.00	1	23/08/2003	£275.00
14	Williams	SN15 3QD	£367.00	2	24/08/2003	£734.00
15	Tipping	SL4 5RF	£262.00	1	25/09/2003	£262.00
16	Trory	ST3 2NJ	£283.00	1	26/09/2003	£283.00
17	Greenslade	BT28 2UH	£342.00	4	27/09/2003	£1,368.00
18	Williams	PR3 2XA	£151.00	4	28/10/2003	£604.00
19	Joudeh	SY161JE	£211.00	5	29/10/2003	£1,055.00
20	Osebor	TW7 4HS	£198.00	2	30/11/2003	£396.00
21	Rothwell	IG11 9AJ	£329.00	2	01/12/2003	£658.00
22	Evans	S11 4HY	£275.00	1	02/12/2003	£275.00
23	Breakey	CH61 6XN	£166.00	2	05/12/2003	£332.00
24	Milton-white	NG319AP	£355.00	2	14/12/2003	£710.00

Record: 1 of 17

Tip:
You can also use the Boolean operators **AND, OR** and **NOT** when using an Internet search engine, for example:
mobile home AND rental AND Italy OR France NOT Normandy
Better still would be **"mobile home"** or **mobile AND home** to exclude phone sites!

O   Close the window.

Note:
Clicking **Save** in Access saves the database design but data is automatically saved when it is entered. In Excel or Word however, any data added is held only in memory and must be manually saved to avoid being lost. There may be a **Save for AutoRecovery** at preset intervals in case of a program crash or power cut.

Exporting data from Access

It would be useful to see the data pictorially as a graph and this can most easily be done in Excel.

To transfer data from an Access table it must be **exported**.

‣ In the database window, with all other windows closed, select **tblBookings**.

‣ From the **File** menu, choose **Export**.

The Export Table dialogue allows you to save a table in a range of formats. The most universal format would be to convert it back to tab-delimited text for any spreadsheet to import. However Access can save it as an Excel file (readable by earlier versions) and this would be the simplest thing to do.

‣ In the **Save in** box find your **ECDL8** folder and in the **Save as type** list scroll down to Microsoft **Excel 97-2002 (*.xls)**.

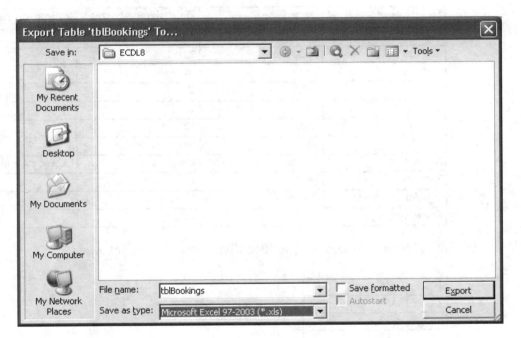

‣ Leave **tblBookings** as the name and click **Export**.

Tip:
Most applications allow you to save work as an earlier version, for backward compatibility.

Access saves the file **tblBookings.xls** in your working folder. This is the end of the Access work.

‣ Close **Access**.

Exercise

In this exercise you are asked to create a database of hotels for the local tourist board guidebook.

1. Download the file **Hotels.txt** from www.payne-gallway.co.uk/ecdl and save it in a new folder called **ECDLexercises**.

2. In Access create a new database called **Hotels.mdb** and save it in your **ECDLexercises** folder.

3. Import the file **Hotels.txt** into a table called **tblhotels** in your new database. The data includes a header row and is tab-delimited. Don't set an ID field.

4. Set the primary key as **HotelRef**.

5. Format the fields in **tblhotels** as follows:

Field Name	Data Type	Field size or Format	Validation rule
HotelRef	Text	5	
Address1	Text	30	
Address2	Text	30	
Town	Text	30	
County	Text	30	
Postcode	Text	10	
Tel	Text	20	
NoBeds	Number	Integer	Between 1 and 100
Pets	Yes/No	1	
DoublePrice	Currency	2 dec. places	
BoardType	Integer	Integer	

6. Make a lookup table for **BoardType** to reflect the following:

1	Self-Cat
2	B&B
3	Half Board
4	Full Board

7. Sort the data in alphabetical order of hotel name.

8. Query the database to find all the hotels that have at least 50 bedrooms and accept pets. Save the query as **qry50bedspluspets**.

9. Export **tblHotels** to an Excel file with the same name in the **ECDLexercises** folder.

10. Close Access

Using Excel

In this chapter you will examine data in a spreadsheet and do some calculations.

Loading Excel

You can so this in one of two ways:

- ◉ *Either* double-click the **Excel** icon on your windows desktop
- ◉ *Or* click **Start** at the bottom left of the screen, then click **Programs**, then

Your screen will look like this:

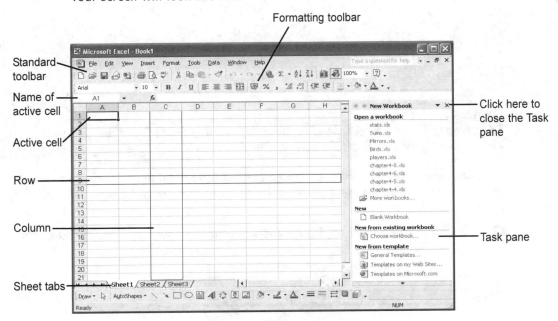

Note:
The Task pane is new in Excel 2002. It lists the workbooks you recently opened and other options. Close it now by clicking the Close icon at the top of the Task pane.

Opening a spreadsheet

You can now open the Bookings spreadsheet saved in the last chapter.

◉ In the Open dialogue window, navigate to your **ECDL8** folder in the **Look in** box and select **tblBookings.xls**. (If you don't see it, check that **Files of type** shows **Microsoft Excel Files**.) Click **Open**.

The data appears in the spreadsheet columns together with the field names, and the worksheet is named **tblBookings**.

◉ Adjust some column widths by double-clicking between the column headers. Dates and numerical data will appear as #### if the column is too narrow.

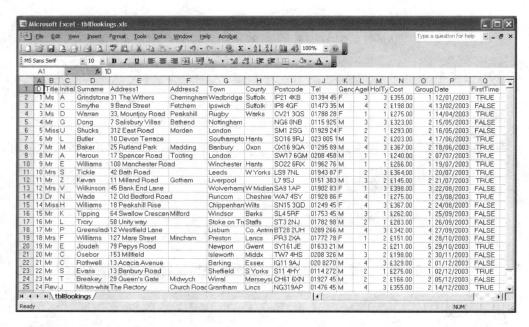

Note:

if you open a comma-delimited or tab-delimited text file in Excel, an Import Wizard prompts you for the data format, just as for Access.

The data here conveniently fits on the screen but if you had much more than this, the column names in the first row would be hidden when you scrolled down. This is easily fixed.

◉ Click the row header for Row 2 and from the **Window** menu select **Freeze Panes**.

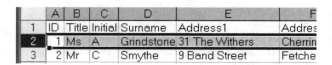

The column names will now stay in view when scrolling.

Data types in Excel

Excel can also set columns or individual cells to handle different types of data. If you had imported the data as a text file, some data types would need to be set but in this case the date and currency columns were set by Access during export. To see the data type of a cell:

⬤ Right-click in one of the **Cost** cells and choose **Format Cells**.

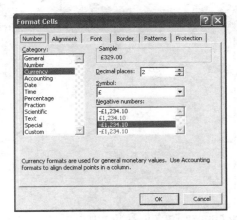

The Format Cells window can also be called up from the **Format** menu, **Cells**. The **Category** list on the left has the available types. **General** accepts numbers or text. The default **Currency** symbol, in this case **£**, is set by Windows from Control Panel but can be changed to **$** or **€**.

⬤ Repeat this in a **Date** cell and a **Number** cell.

Notice the date can be displayed in different ways, such as **dd/mm/yy** or **yyyy-mm-dd**. (The USA commonly uses **mm/dd/yyyy**.) Numbers can have decimal places and be shown in red if negative.

Lookup tables

The **AgeRange** and **HolType** field values look unfriendly as codes but as in Access this can be remedied with lookup tables. These can be put on the same sheet, another worksheet or even a different workbook. The lookup values need new columns.

⬤ First select the **HolType** column by clicking the column header and choose **Insert**, **Columns**.

This makes a new column for the **AgeRange** lookup. We'll put the lookup table on the current sheet.

⬤ Click in the cell **T1** and type **Age Range lookup**.

⬤ Enter the values shown.

It is a good idea to give a **Name** to a range of cells. This makes formulae easier to read and allows you to move the table or extend it.

●   Click in the table and press **Ctrl-Shift-*** to select the entire table.

●   Click in the **Name Box** at the left of the Formula bar and name the table **AgeRangeLookup**. Press **Enter**.

●   In cell **M1** enter the title **Age**.

●   Click in cell **M2** and click the **Insert Function** button **fx**.

The Insert Function window appears.

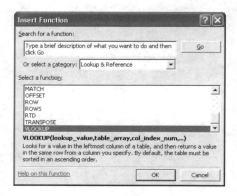

●   In the **Or select a category** box, choose **Lookup & Reference**. From the **Select a function** box, select **VLOOKUP**. Click **OK**.

●   In the VLOOKUP dialogue box, enter the values shown below.

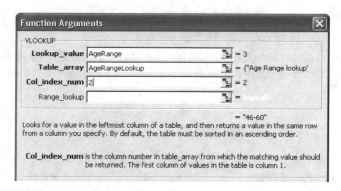

●   Click **OK**.

Cell M2 now has a value calculated as shown in the Formula bar.

fx =VLOOKUP(AgeRange,AgeRangeLookup,2)

●   Click on the cell and drag the corner handle right down the column to copy the formula. Each cell should have the matching age range for the code.

●   In the same way make a new column for the **HolType** lookup, called **Holiday** and a lookup table in Columns **X** and **Y** (as shown) with the name **HolidayLookup**. Fill in the VLOOKUP values in the dialogue and copy the formula down the column.

Calculated fields

Just as in Access, the total value of a booking can be calculated from the unit cost and number of people.

- Select the **Date** column and choose **Insert, Column**.

- Give the column the name **Amount** in R1.

- In **R2** type **=P2*Q2** and press **Enter**.

The product of **Cost** and **Group** appears in the cell.

- Select the cell and drag the handle in its lower right-hand corner down the column to copy the formula.

Notice Excel adjusts the row number in the formula for each row, so that in cell **R3**, the formula is **=P3*Q3**. You may need to widen the column.

- Try changing the value in cell **P3** to **£100** and notice the value in cell **R3** automatically changes. Click **Undo** to undo this change.

The spreadsheet should now look something like this. (You will need to adjust some column widths.)

ID	Title	Initi	Surname	Address1	Addres	Town	County	Postcode	Tel	Ger	Age	Age	HolTy	Holiday	Cost	Group	Amount	Date	Firs
1	Ms	A	Grindstone	31 The Wit	Cherrin	Wadbridge	Suffolk	IP21 4KB	0139	F	3	46-60	3	Cruise	£355.00	1	£355.00	12/01/2003	TF
2	Mr	C	Smythe	9 Band Stre	Fetcher	Ipswich	Suffolk	IP8 4GF	0147	M	4	Over 60	2	Beach	£198.00	4	£792.00	13/02/2003	FA
3	Ms	D	Warren	33, Mountjo	Peaksh	Rugby	Warks	CV21 3QS	0178	F	1	18-29	1	Activity	£275.00	1	£275.00	14/04/2003	TF
4	Mr	G	Dong	7 Salisbury	Bathen	Nottingham		NG6 0NB	0115	M	3	46-60	3	Cruise	£323.00	2	£646.00	15/05/2003	FA
5	Miss	U	Shucks	312 East R	Morden	London		SM1 2SG	0192	F	2	30-45	1	Activity	£293.00	2	£586.00	16/05/2003	FA
6	Mr	L	Butler	10 Devon Terrace	Southampto	Hants		SO16 9RJ	0231	M	2	30-45	2	Beach	£203.00	4	£812.00	17/06/2003	TF
7	Mr	M	Baker	25 Rutland	Maddin	Banbury	Oxon	OX16 9QA	0129	M	4	Over 60	3	Cruise	£367.00	2	£734.00	18/06/2003	TF
8	Mr	A	Haroun	17 Spencer	Tooting	London		SW17 6GM	0208	M	1	18-29	1	Activity	£240.00	2	£480.00	07/07/2003	TF
9	Mr	E	Williams	100 Manchester Ro	Winchester	Hants		SO22 6RX	0198	M	1	18-29	1	Activity	£266.00	1	£266.00	19/07/2003	TF
10	Mrs	S	Tickle	42 Bath Road	Leeds	W Yorks		LS9 7NL	0194	F	2	30-45	3	Cruise	£364.00	1	£364.00	20/07/2003	TF
11	Mr	Z	Kevan	11 Milland	Gotham	Liverpool		L7 9SJ	0151	M	3	46-60	2	Beach	£145.00	2	£290.00	21/07/2003	TF
12	Mrs	V	Wilkinson	45 Bank End Lane	Wolverhamp	W Midlan		SA9 1AP	0190	F	1	18-29	3	Cruise	£398.00	3	£1,194.00	22/08/2003	FA
13	Dr	N	Wade	12 Old Bedford Roa	Runcorn	Cheshire		WA7 4SY	0192	F	4	Over 60	1	Activity	£275.00	1	£275.00	23/08/2003	TF
14	Miss	H	Williams	18 Peakshill Rise	Chippenhan	Wilts		SN15 3QD	0124	F	4	Over 60	3	Cruise	£367.00	2	£734.00	24/08/2003	FA
15	Mr	K	Tipping	64 Swallow	Milford	Windsor	Berks	SL4 5RF	0175	M	3	46-60	1	Activity	£262.00	1	£262.00	25/09/2003	FA
16	Mr	L	Trory	58 Unity way	Stoke on Tr	Staffs		ST3 2NJ	0178	M	2	30-45	1	Activity	£283.00	1	£283.00	26/09/2003	FA
17	Mr	P	Greenslad	12 Westfield Lane	Lisburn	Co. Antrin		BT28 2UH	0289	M	4	Over 60	3	Cruise	£342.00	4	£1,368.00	27/09/2003	FA
18	Mrs	F	Williams	127 Mare S	Minchar	Preston	Lancs	PR3 2XA	0177	F	1	18-29	2	Beach	£151.00	4	£604.00	28/10/2003	FA
19	Mr	E	Joudeh	79 Pepys Road	Newport	Gwent		SY161JE	0163	M	1	18-29	2	Beach	£211.00	5	£1,055.00	29/10/2003	TF
20	Mr	C	Osebor	153 Millfield	Isleworth	Middx		TW7 4HS	0208	M	3	46-60	2	Beach	£198.00	2	£396.00	30/11/2003	FA
21	Mr	C	Rothwell	13 Acacia Avenue	Barking	Essex		IG11 9AJ	0201	M	4	Over 60	3	Cruise	£329.00	2	£658.00	01/12/2003	FA
22	Mr	S	Evans	13 Banbury Road	Sheffield	S Yorks		S11 4HY	0114	M	2	30-45	1	Activity	£275.00	1	£275.00	02/12/2003	TF
23	Mr	T	Breakey	29 Queen's	Midwyc	Wirral	Merseysi	CH61 6XN	0192	M	2	30-45	2	Beach	£166.00	2	£332.00	05/12/2003	FA
24	Rev	J	Milton-white	The Rector	Church	Grantham	Lincs	NG319AP	0147	M	4	Over 60	3	Cruise	£355.00	2	£710.00	14/12/2003	TF

Other calculations

It would be useful to know the total of all the bookings.

- Scroll down the **Cost** column (**P**) and in the third cell below the last record type **Grand Total**. This needs to stand out so make it bold.

- In the same row click in the **Amount** column and click the **AutoSum** button on the toolbar.

Excel surrounds all the cells above with a moving dotted line and puts the formula for the SUM function in the cell.

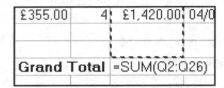

£355.00	4	£1,420.00	04/0
Grand Total	=SUM(Q2:Q26)		

- ▶ Press **Enter** to show the sum of all the numbers as the grand total. Note the range of cells used for the SUM.

It would also be useful to know the average cost per booking, and to calculate this there is the **AVERAGE** function.

> **Tip:**
> When a cell with a calculated value is selected, the actual formula is shown in the Formula bar at the top.

- ▶ In the cell below **Grand Total** type **Average** and make it bold.
- ▶ In the same row in the **Amount** column type **=average(R2:R27)** and press **Enter**.

The average booking amount should be shown.

> **Note:**
> The range of cells used above includes two blank cells. Sometimes it may happen that blank cells have been filled with zeroes: this will not affect the sum but it will affect the average, since the total has not changed but the number of cells with numerical data has. This also affects the COUNT function: look up what this does.

- ▶ Now type zero into a blank cell above the grand total, click out of the cell and notice the difference! Click **Undo** to undo your latest change.

Data modelling

The big advantage of an electronic spreadsheet is that a cell can be given a reference to another cell rather than a specific value. This is very useful for modelling and projecting the effect of changing a value (such as cost) since all the values which depend on it change instantly.

To trace which cells are dependent on others:

- ▶ Click in a cell and choose **Tools, Formula Auditing, Trace Dependents**.

3	Cruise	£355.00	2	£710.00
		Grand Total		£13,471.00
		Average		£585.70

> **Tip:**
> Formulae should be entered left to right and top to bottom.

Adding data

Another booking has come in that you want to add to this batch.

Title	Mrs	Gender	F
Initials	J	AgeRange	2
Surname	Higgins	HolType	2
Address1	32 Elgin Close	Cost	191
Address2		Group	2
Town	Wolverhampton	Date	18/12/2003
Postcode	WV5 3KB	FirstTime	TRUE

◉   Add these details to the first free row (with 25 for **ID**).

◉   **Age**, **Holiday** and **Amount** will be blank if the calculations were not copied to this row. If so, copy it for each from the cell above.

Notice the sum and average will also change.

When typing in **Wolverhampton** you may have noticed that after the first two or three characters the rest of the word suddenly appears, highlighted: to accept this you just tab out of the cell. If however you really wanted Wolfenden, carry on typing.

Tip:

It is often best to enter data in Excel since it compares what you type with what is already in that column and presents a match: no need then to keep typing Newcastle Upon Tyne or Machynlleth in full – just start off and Excel completes it for you!

Sorting data

The bookings are currently in the order originally entered; that is, date (and ID). To see which are worth most we could put them into Amount order.

◉   Click anywhere in the **Amount** column and click **Sort Ascending**.

The records are now in order of lowest to highest **Amount**.

Tip:

To see the highest first, click **Sort Descending**.

It is often useful to have several levels of sorting. If you were looking at responses from different parts of the country you would sort by county, then town, then surname. In the bookings records, sorting will reveal relationships between age and type of holiday.

◉   Click anywhere in the record list and choose **Data, Sort**.

Excel highlights all the cells except the header row.

Note:

Excel will recognise there is a header row if some data is numeric. If it does not, however, the header row will disappear – to be found sorted amongst the other records, thus corrupting your data. It is important to be aware of this.

The Sort dialogue box allows you to enter up to three sort fields.

▶ Enter **HolType**, then **AgeRange**, then **Date**, and click **OK**.

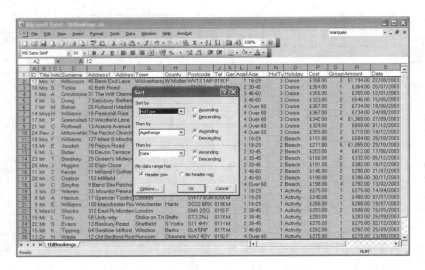

The records now show the age ranges by date for each activity. One could do further analysis with more sort levels but Excel only has three.

Caution:

When sorting, Excel selects the block of cells with data surrounding the active cell, otherwise it sorts a range of cells that has been selected. If however you sort with a column selected, only that column will be sorted. This means that if you sort on postcode with that column selected, the postcodes are reshuffled and all the records will have the wrong postcode. The data will then have lost its integrity, and if you save the file it will be almost unusable.

Sorting in Excel is not case-sensitive but in some applications it is, so that

Ants		Ants
bees	becomes	Cows
Cows		bees

Searching in Excel

You can find data in Excel in much the same way as for **Find** in Access.

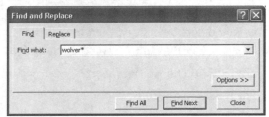

▶ To find all the records containing Wolverhampton, choose **Edit**, **Find** (or press **Ctrl-F**).

▶ Enter **Wolverhampton**, or **Wolver*** if you want to use wildcards.

Selecting a range of cells or a column will search that area only. **Options** lets you match the case and **Find All** lists all the occurrences below. **Replace** will change an item and is useful if for example a changed phone code needs to be changed throughout.

 Save your spreadsheet.

Exercise

In this exercise you will develop the data on hotels that you imported into an Excel spreadsheet at the end of Chapter 2.

1. Open the file **Hotels.xls** in the **ECDLexercises** folder.

2. Insert a new column Board.

3. Use the VLOOKUP function to insert the board arrangements offered by the hotels into the new column. The lookup table should contain the following values:

1	Sel-Cat
2	B&B
3	Half Board
4	Full Board

4. Insert another new column entitled **OffPeakDoublePrice**. The entries in this new column reflect the price of a double room during the Off Peak season. During this time prices are reduced by 15%. Complete the entries for this new column.

5. Add a new hotel to the spreadsheet.

HotelRef	H21
Address1	The Havens
Address2	High Street
Town	Bindham
County	Essex
Postcode	CM23 8UJ
Tel	01226 674256
NoBeds	45
Pets	No
DoublePrice	£37.50
BoardType	2

6. Sort the data into ascending order of price and then alphabetically by hotel name.

7. Save the spreadsheet and close Excel.

CHAPTER

4

Charts

Charts are a way to present information pictorially so that trends and relationships stand out and are easy to grasp.

For example, we could find the proportion of the total holiday revenue coming from each age group and holiday type. To do this we need Excel to show the subtotal of **Amount** for each value of **AgeRange**.

Subtotals

The records must be in order of age range.

▶ Click anywhere in the **AgeRange** column and click **Sort Ascending**.

▶ Select **Data, Subtotals** and fill in the Subtotal dialogue box as below.

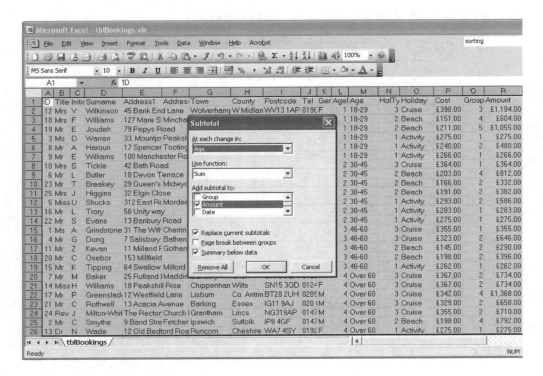

◉   Click **OK**.

There are now 4 subtotal rows showing the **Amount** subtotal for each value of **Age**. (Using Age makes it more meaningful than AgeRange.)

Outline —
buttons

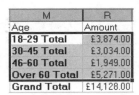

Tip:
The subtotals are shown selected here but you don't have to do that yet.

◉   Click the Outline button **2** at top left to show the totals only.

◉   Now drag to select columns **N** to **Q**, right-click on the selected area and choose **Hide**.

The **Age** and **Amount** columns are now next to each other.

Pie charts

The Chart Wizard plots a chart from any data you have highlighted.

◉   Drag to select the totals and amounts (but not **Grand Total**) in a block.

M	R
Age	Amount
18-29 Total	£3,874.00
30-45 Total	£3,034.00
46-60 Total	£1,949.00
Over 60 Total	£5,271.00
Grand Total	£14,128.00

◉   Click on the **Chart Wizard** button on the Standard toolbar.

The Chart Wizard lists the available chart types on the left and illustrates the subtypes for each.

▶ Select **Pie**.

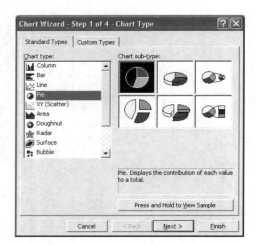

Note:
Similar to the Pie is the **Doughnut**.

▶ Click **Press and Hold to View Sample** to preview the chart.

▶ Now have a look at the other types of pie chart and click to view samples.

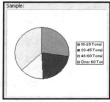

We'll make the 3-D exploded pie chart in the middle of the lower row.

▶ With this chart selected, click **Next** then **Next** again and give the chart the title **Revenue by Age Group**.

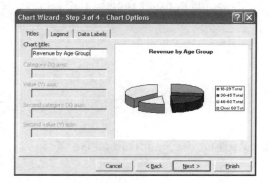

The **legend** on the right is the key to what each slice of the pie represents.

▶ Click the **Legend** tab and try moving the legend, or removing it.

The pie could do with some values.

▶ On the **Data Labels** tab, click **Value** to add the subtotals.

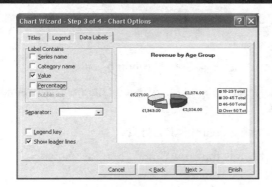

Note:
You could also add the percentage made up by each slice. Remember a pie chart can only be used where the values are proportions of a whole.

● Click **Next**, select **As object in** then **Finish**.

The final chart appears in the spreadsheet. Moving the mouse pointer over it will show tool tips explaining the parts of the chart. The Chart toolbar lets you make changes.

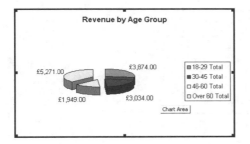

Drag the chart to move it, or Shift-drag a corner handle to size it.

It would be useful to make another chart with different subtotals using a copy of the data.

● Save your spreadsheet by clicking the **Save** button (or **Ctrl-S**).

● Now choose **File, Save As**, change the file name to **tblBookings2.xls** and click **Save**.

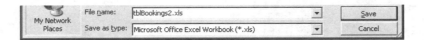

First we need to show the data again.

● Remove the chart by selecting it and pressing **Delete**.

● Select columns **M** and **R**, right-click and choose **Unhide**.

● Click Outline button **3** at top left to show all the data.

● Click in the data, choose **Data, Subtotals** and click **Remove All**.

We can now choose different subtotals.

● Click in the **Holiday** column and click **Sort Ascending**.

● Choose **Data, Subtotals** and set **Holiday** for **At each change in** and **Amount** for **Add subtotal to**. Click **OK**.

● Click Outline button **2** and hide columns **P** and **Q**.

● Drag to select the new subtotals (but not Grand Total) as shown.

O	R
Holiday	Amount
Activity Total	£2,702.00
Beach Total	£4,663.00
Cruise Total	£6,763.00
Grand Total	£14,128.00

● Now use the Chart Wizard to make another exploded pie chart as before, give it the title **Revenue by Holiday Type** and embed it in the spreadsheet as before.

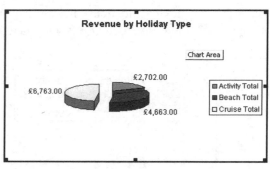

● Save your spreadsheet.

Other types of chart

You could have chosen a **column chart** or a **bar chart** to show the same information.

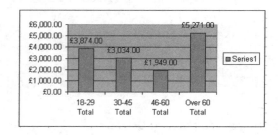
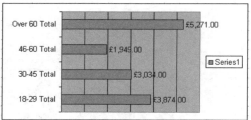

A **line chart** is not suitable for this data, being used to show a trend over time – for example rising (or falling) sales figures over a period of months or years.

XY scatter graphs are generally used when the points are too numerous and scattered to be joined up, such as with scientific or statistical data. The shape of the cluster can be used to find a correlation or prove a theory.

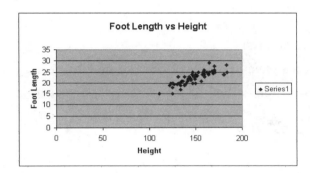

This almost completes our work with Excel, but not quite.

Exercise

The Tourist Board would like to use the spreadsheet you created in the practice exercise at the end of Chapter 3 to analyse the types of hotel accomodation available in the area.

1.   Open the spreadsheet **Hotels.xls** which should be in the **ECDLexercises** folder.

2.   Sort the data by **Board**.

3.   Insert subtotals which count the number of hotels in each board category (you will have to select the **Count** function in the **Subtotal** dialogue box).

4.   Create a pie chart to show what proportion of the hotels listed offer each type of board arrangements. Add appropriate titles and data labels.

5.   Insert the chart into the worksheet below the data.

6.   Remove the subtotals and repeat steps 2-5 above to create a pie chart showing the number of hotels that accept pets

7.   Save the spreadsheet and close Excel.

Having manipulated the data in Access and Excel, it is now time to see how it can be transferred to a word processor.

CHAPTER 5

Using Word

Opening Word

You can do this in one of two ways:

◉ *Either* double-click the **Word** icon on your windows desktop

◉ *Or* click **Start** at the bottom-left of the screen, then click **Programs**, then click

> ☑ Microsoft Office Word 2003

The opening screen

Your opening screen will look something like this:

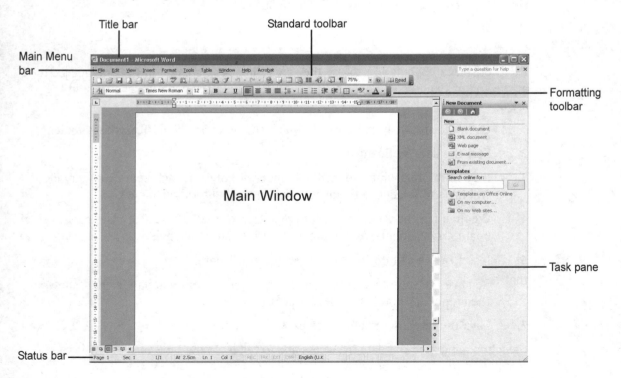

Starting a new document

With Word open, you should have a blank page entitled something like **Document 1**.

 ❍ If you don't have this, click **Blank Document** on the toolbar.

We are going to write two documents:

❶ A report to head office

❶ An offer to existing customers

❍ Type in the following skeleton of a report. There are bits missing.

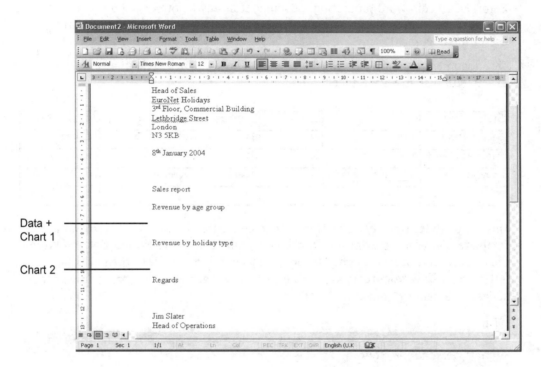

Data + Chart 1

Chart 2

Using Styles

A **style** is defined as a set of formatting characteristics such as typeface, size and weight. Styles are used to maintain a consistent look throughout a long document. For example, you might create one style for chapter headings, another for paragraph headings and a third for the 'body text'. Word has some default styles already set up.

As you start to type in a new Word document, you can see from the Formatting toolbar that the text is **Times New Roman**, size **12** pt (unless someone has changed this on your computer), and aligned to the left. The Style box at the left of the toolbar shows **Normal** – this is the name given to the default style in Word.

 ❍ Click on the down arrow to see the other built-in styles in a new document.

The subject of the letter needs to stand out. We could make it bigger and in bold but both operations can be done in one by applying a style.

- ◉ Click in the line **Sales report**, open the Styles list and choose **Heading 1**.

- ◉ Oops – too big! Try **Heading 2** instead and make the next two headings **Heading 3**.

A major advantage of using styles is that if you decide, after typing the document, that you want all the headings in a different size or font, you can simply change the style and all the headings will automatically adopt the new style characteristics.

Creating your own styles

Before you begin word processing a document of any length or importance, such as a formal report, you should create a **style sheet** which lists all the styles you are going to use in the document.

This document itself may be word processed, showing each style in a table. Here is an example of a simple style sheet:

Style name	Font	Size	Emphasis	Spacing	Justification
Section Head	Arial	24	Bold, underlined	12pt before	Centred
Paragraph Head	Arial	16	Bold	6pt before	Left
Body Text	Times New Roman	11	Plain	None	Left
etc					

This set of styles (the style sheet) may then be created in Word and stored in a **template** file with the extension **.dot**. The default template is **Normal.dot** and Word provides several others which you can see by choosing **File**, **New**, then clicking on a letter under **New from template** on the Task pane. Each template has its own set of styles. Web pages also use style sheets.

> **Tip:**
> You can print the styles in the current template using **File**, **Print**. In the **Print what:** box choose **Styles**.

Emphasising data

Important data needs emphasis so as to stand out. This can be done with styles or by applying the formatting directly. Ways of emphasising include **bold**, *italic*, underline (except on web pages, where it looks like a link), **font**, **colour** (where visible), bulleted lists or numbered paragraphs as used in this book.

Headers and footers

Headers (not headings) and footers are areas at the top and bottom of the page where you can put text and graphics which are to appear on each page in the document. Our document needs the company title in the header and a page number in the footer since it will be more than one page.

○ From the **View** menu choose **Header and Footer**.

The Header box appears, and the Header and Footer toolbar.

○ Click in the **Header** box, select **Heading 1** in the style box and type the text below.

 ○ On the Header and Footer toolbar, click **Switch Between Header and Footer** to show the **Footer** box.

 ○ Press **Tab** to put the page number in the centre and click **Insert Page Number** on the toolbar.

This inserts a field – that is to say, a placeholder that puts the page number at that place on each page. You can tell it is a field as it appears grey when you click on it. As well the page number, a report needs to show how many pages are in the report.

 ○ Click after the page number and type a space followed by **of** then another space. Now click **Insert Number of Pages**.

Tip:
Click **Insert AutoText** on the toolbar to see what else could go in a header or footer.

○ Click **Close** on the Header and Footer toolbar.

Inserting data from Excel

The report is now ready except for the information to go in it, in the spaces labelled Data and Chart in the figure earlier in this chapter. First the data.

○ Open **tblBookings.xls** in Excel and find the Pie Chart data.

○ Drag to select all the data cells and the Grand Total and choose **Edit, Copy** (or press **Ctrl-C**) to copy the cells to the clipboard.

Note:
The **clipboard** is an area of memory available to all applications which allows you to copy, cut and paste all kinds of data.

● Now return to your Word document (select it in the Task bar or press **Alt–Tab**) and click where the data is to go.

● Choose **Edit, Paste** (or press **Ctrl-V**).

The data will look like this:

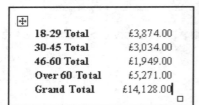

18-29 Total	£3,874.00
30-45 Total	£3,034.00
46-60 Total	£1,949.00
Over 60 Total	£5,271.00
Grand Total	£14,128.00

Tip:
When you copy a range of cells from **Excel** to **Word**, they appear as a table. You can do the same from **Access** in datasheet view: to select the values, click in the first field to be copied then shift-click the last field of the range.

Inserting a chart

● Below the table, type **As a chart this looks like:**

● Switch to Excel, click near the edge of the pie chart to select the whole chart and press **Ctrl-C**.

● Switch back to Word, click on the next line, and choose **Edit, Paste Special**.

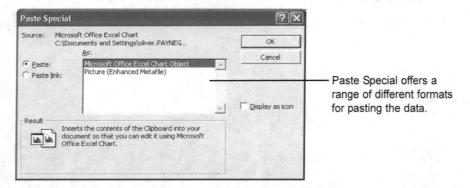

Paste Special offers a range of different formats for pasting the data.

● Click **Paste** and press **OK**.

● The chart appears in Word. Select it and drag a corner handle to make it smaller.

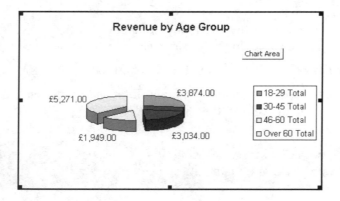

When sizing an image, always drag a handle at a corner not on a side (in some applications you may need **Shift** as well) or the image will lose its original proportions (**aspect ratio**) and be distorted, like this:

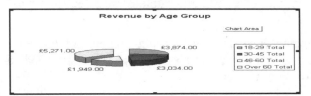

◑ In the next space in your letter, copy and paste the chart in **tblBookings2.xls** in the same way but using the option **Paste link**.

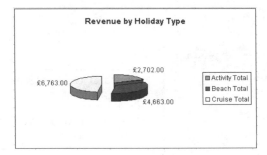

◑ Save your file as **Report.doc**.

Embedded and linked objects

Paste Special inserts an **Excel Chart** as either an **embedded object** or a **linked object**. In both cases Word is actually storing a link to Excel. A normal **Paste** gives no connection to Excel.

Tip:

You can see the link by selecting a chart in Word and pressing **Shift-F9**. It will look something like this:

{ LINK Excel.Sheet.8 "C:\\Documents and Settings\\oliver.Pg\\My Documents\\ECDL8\\tblBookings2.xls" "tblBookings![tblBookings2.xls]tblBookings Chart 1" \a \p * MERGEFORMAT }

Press it again to restore the chart.

Double-clicking an embedded object opens the chart since it is a copy of the original data whereas double-clicking a linked object opens the original spreadsheet. Any changes made to a chart in Excel will also appear in a linked (but not an embedded) object, so that if a late change has to be made to the chart there is no need to correct it in the report.

Tip:

To see this, go to **tblBookings2.xls**, change the Cruise total to £10,000, press Enter and notice the chart changes. Back in **Report.doc** right-click on the second chart and choose **Update Field** (or you could select it and press **F9**) – the chart should change. Return to Excel and click **Undo**!

Mail merge

Mail merge allows you to personalise a letter you are sending to many people, by inserting individual names, addresses and other details imported from a database or spreadsheet.

In this case, the management have decided that more people in the age ranges below 60 might be induced to take a cruise at a time when there is spare capacity. You will send a special offer to these customers.

▶ Create a new blank Word document.

You could type the date in full but it is sometimes convenient to enter the date as a field that Word updates every time the document is opened.

▶ Choose **Insert, Date and Time**.

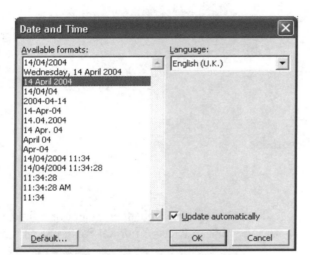

The date for a letter should have the month name and the year in full. It will update if the **Update Automatically** box is checked.

▶ Choose a suitable format and click **OK**.

▶ Insert about 10 blank lines then enter the following text.

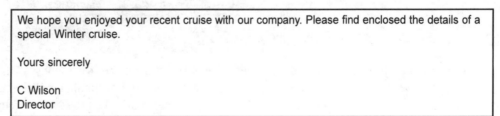

We hope you enjoyed your recent cruise with our company. Please find enclosed the details of a special Winter cruise.

Yours sincerely

C Wilson
Director

▶ Save the letter as **CruiseOffer.doc**

The letter will need mail merge fields in the address area. Mail Merge can use data from Excel or Access: in this case the query **qryCruise** has the required data or you could do a conditional mail merge.

Next we need to place the mail merge fields in the address area of the letter. We shall use the Mail Merge toolbar rather than the wizard as in Module 3.

○ From the menu bar, choose **View**, **Toolbars**, **Mail Merge** to show the Mail Merge toolbar.

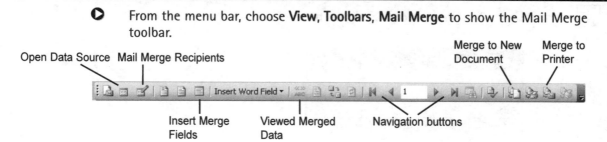

Open Data Source Mail Merge Recipients

Merge to New Document Merge to Printer

Insert Merge Fields Viewed Merged Data Navigation buttons

○ Click **Open Data Source** on the toolbar and in the dialogue box click **My Documents**, find your **Bookings.mdb** file and click **Open**.

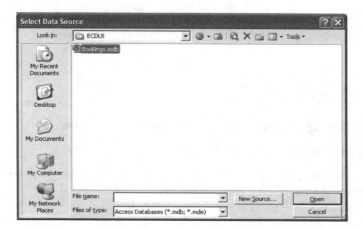

○ In the Select Table dialogue, choose **qryCruise** and click OK

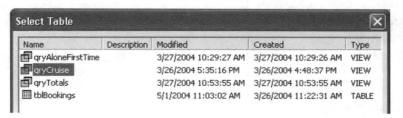

○ Click the **Mail Merge Recipients** button to see the records selected by **qryCruise**. (You could remove some records here if you wished.)

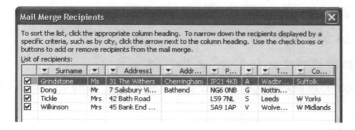

○ Click **OK** to close the window and click at the top of the address area, below the date.

◉ Click **Insert Merge Fields** on the toolbar.

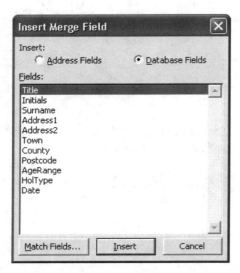

◉ Double-click on each field down to **Postcode** then click **Close**.

You now have a continuous line of merge fields.

◉ Space out the fields as shown and copy and edit the first line to make the greetings line. Remove any excess space below.

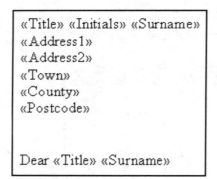

 ◉ Click **View Merged Data** on the toolbar and browse the records with the navigation buttons.

◉ Save your document.

The letters can now be printed out.

 ◉ Click **Merge to Printer** on the toolbar, then **OK**.

Alternatively you could click **Merge to New Document** to preview the letters before printing.

Searching in Word

Finding and replacing characters, words or phrases in Word is very fast.

◐   Select **Edit**, **Find** or **Replace**.

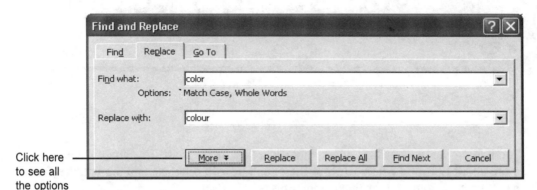

Click here
to see all
the options

You can match the case and find whole words as well as styles and formatting. Wildcards can be used. **Replace All** replaces all occurrences in any text selected or the whole document.

Exercise

Having produced the charts analysing the facilities provided by hotels in the local area at the end of Chapter 4, you are now required to insert these charts into a short report for the Manager of the Tourist Board.

1.   Open a new Word document and save it as **Hotels.doc** in the **ECDLexercises** folder.

2.   Type in the skeleton of a report that includes the following headings:

    Analysis of local hotels

    Introduction

    Board arrangements offered by hotels

    Hotels accepting guests accompanied by pets

    Conclusion

3.   Insert the date as a field which will be automatically updated.

4.   Insert a header **Hotel Report** and a footer that contains the page number which should be centred.

5.   Enter a small amount of text into the **Introduction** and **Conclusion** sections.

6.   Insert the two charts from the file **Hotels.xls** (created at the end of Chapter 4) into the appropriate places in the report.

7.   In a separate document create a style sheet for this report.

8.   Apply the styles specified on the style sheet to the document.

CHAPTER 6

Managing Files

You had a brief view of files when importing data at the start. This chapter tells you more about files and where to store them; and how to organise and manipulate them, back them up, and protect them from viruses.

Creating and naming files

You have already created files in Access, Excel and Word. A file name can be up to 255 characters long, including spaces. While there's generally no need for a name this long, it is a good idea to have a meaningful name that will be easily identified later, such as **Tax 2004** rather than just **Letter**.

File names are given an **extension** of a dot followed by usually 3 characters. Apart from being a convenient label, this serves to tell Windows which program to open a file in when you double-click on the name. If Windows has no **association** for a file type, it prompts you to choose a program.

File types

The file type depends on which application the file was created in. Here are some examples of common file types:

.doc	a word-processed file produced in MS Word
.xls	a spreadsheet produced in MS Excel
.mdb	a database created in MS Access
.ppt	a presentation created in MS PowerPoint
.pub	a desktop publishing file created in MS Publisher
.bmp	a bitmapped graphic created in a graphics package
.jpg, .gif, .tif, .wmf	different types of graphics file
.mp3, .mid, .wav	an audio file
.avi, .mpeg, .mov	a video file
.htm	a web page file
.zip	a compressed file
.tmp	a temporary file
.exe	a program (executable) file

Storing files

Putting all your files in the same place rapidly leads to confusion so it is important to organise your files into **folders,** which may in turn contain subfolders. Windows sets up a folder **My Documents** which is where it expects you to save your files, for example:

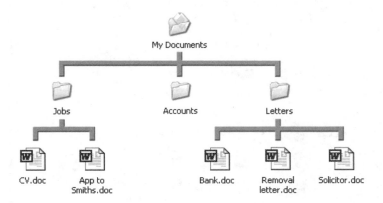

Where files are stored

There are several locations where files might be stored on a computer.

 ◉   Click the **Start** button to show the Start menu.

The familiar picture screen with a few icons is known as the **Desktop**.

◉   Click on **My Computer**.

The My Computer window gives an overview of the machine.

Drives

In the right-hand pane are all the disk drives associated with the computer.

The main **Hard Disk Drive** is **Local Disk (C:)**. Sometimes a hard disk is **partitioned** into two or more **logical** drives, which would be **D:**, **E:**, and so on. Hard disks currently hold up to 80Gb (Gigabytes) of data or more.

Among the **Devices with Removable Storage** there is generally a **Floppy (A:)** drive. A floppy disk holds up to 1.44Mb.

On the machine shown above there is also a **Zip** drive (**D:**) holding up to 250Mb, and two **CD** (compact disk) drives (**E:**) and (**F:**), one read-only and one to read or write data. CDs hold 650Mb or more. Increasingly used are **DVD** (Digital Versatile Disk) drives, holding many times more than a CD.

Under **Network Drives** are shown any computers or File Servers the computer is connected to. A network drive may be **mapped** to any letter you like, such as **P:** or **Q:**. This is convenient for documents with linked files (such as charts or pictures) because the linked file **pathname** will then be correct for any machine opening the document provided that it has the drive mapped correctly.

Creating a folder

◉ Click on **My Documents** under **Other Places**.

In **My Documents** are some other general folders (such as **My Music**, **My Pictures**) set up by Windows. There is also the folder **ECDL8** which you created earlier. Notice **Other Places** now lists the **Desktop** (which is actually a folder).

◉ Click **Make a new folder** under the **File and Folder Tasks**.

◉ Type **Working** in the **New Folder** text and press **Enter**.

Copying, moving and deleting files and folders

The new folder needs to go into ECDL8.

○ Select **Working** and click **Move this folder** in the tasks list.

○ Select **ECDL8** and click **Move**.

○ Double-click the ECDL8 folder to see the new folder in it.

○ Click **Back** to return to **My Documents**.

○ Now make a new folder **Tmp** and move it into **Working**.

○ Select the file **Bookings.txt** and copy it to **Working**.

○ In **Working**, move it to **Tmp**.

○ Double-click **Tmp** and rename the file to **Import Old.txt**.

Note:
If you try and change the file extension – for example, changing .txt to .doc – Windows will warn you that this could make the file unusable.

○ Now select the file and click **Delete this file**.

Recycle Bin

Deleted files are placed in a special folder called the **Recycle Bin** which you can see on the Desktop. If you delete a file (or folder) by mistake, you can recover it again by double-clicking **Recycle Bin** to show the files, right-clicking the file and choosing **Restore**.

○ To empty the Recycle Bin, right-click the icon and choose **Empty Recycle Bin**. Nothing can be recovered now!

Note:
Files deleted from a floppy disk or network drive are permanently deleted and not sent to the Recycle Bin.

Searching for files

If you forget where a file is, or perhaps need to find all the files of a certain type created in a particular year, **My Computer** has a **Search** facility.

◉ Open **My Computer** and click the **Search** button.

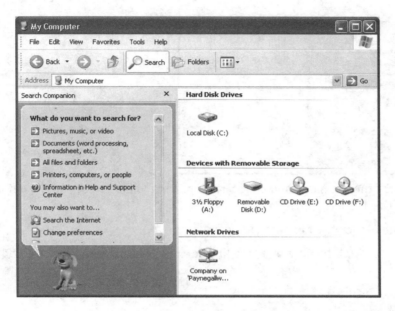

We'll look for the letter **CruiseOffer.doc** which you made earlier.

◉ Click on **Documents** in the list on the left, type the name and click **Search**.

Windows has found the file.

● Select the file name and click **Search** in the toolbar to see the file details at the foot of the left pane.

● Double-click the file name to open it.

You can also search for files by name (including wildcards), date, file size and contents.

● Close the window.

Other views in Windows Explorer

Opening Windows Explorer directly instead of from My Computer can give a different view of the files, as in earlier Windows versions.

● Right-click the **Start** button and choose **Explore**.

Note:

You could also use **Start**, **All Programs**, **Accessories**, **Windows Explorer**, or **Windows** key plus **E**.

● Choose **View**, **Details** and check the **Folders** button is selected.

◑ Select **Tools, Folder Options**, set **Use Windows classic folders** then on the **View** tab make the settings as follows.

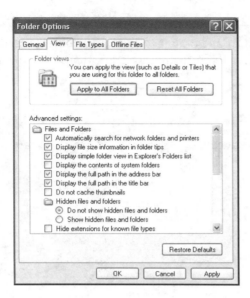

◑ Click **Apply to all Folders** and confirm, then **OK**.

A folder of files will look something like this.

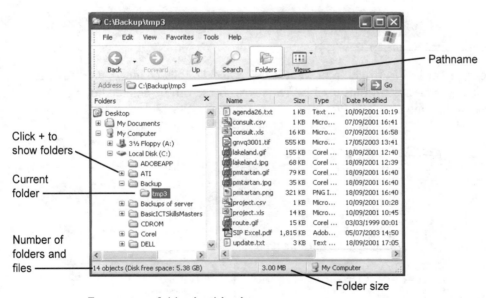

To create a folder in this view:

◑ Click the parent folder in the left pane and select **File, New, Folder**. Edit the **New Folder** name and press **Enter**.

Tip:

Pressing the **F2** key lets you rename a file or folder.

To move a file or folder:

◉ Select the item and drag it to the target folder (or select **Edit**, **Move to Folder**).

To copy a file or folder:

◉ Select the item, hold down **Ctrl** and drag it to the target folder (or select **Edit**, **Copy to Folder**). If you are copying it to another drive, there is no need to press **Ctrl**.

File and folder properties

The network administrator can give **access rights** to selected users to share a drive, folder or file.

A file can be set to **Read-only** to prevent it being accidentally changed, or **Hidden** to hide it (usually for **system** files used by Windows). These can be changed by right-clicking the file and choosing **Properties**.

Sorting files

Files can be sorted by name, size, date or type.

Click on a header to sort; click again to reverse the order.

Name ▲	Size	Date Modifi
agenda26.txt	1 KB	10/09/2001
consult.csv	1 KB	07/09/2001
consult.xls	16 KB	07/09/2001
gnvq3001.tif	555 KB	17/05/2003
lakeland.gif	155 KB	18/09/2001
lakeland.jpg	68 KB	18/09/2001
pmtartan.gif	79 KB	18/09/2001
pmtartan.jpg	35 KB	18/09/2001
pmtartan.png	321 KB	18/09/2001
project.csv	1 KB	10/09/2001
project.xls	14 KB	10/09/2001
route.gif	15 KB	03/03/1999
SIP Excel.pdf	1,815 KB	05/07/2003
update.txt	3 KB	18/09/2001

Name	Size ▲	Date Modifi
project.csv	1 KB	10/09/2001
agenda26.txt	1 KB	10/09/2001
consult.csv	1 KB	07/09/2001
update.txt	3 KB	18/09/2001
project.xls	14 KB	10/09/2001
route.gif	15 KB	03/03/1999
consult.xls	16 KB	07/09/2001
pmtartan.jpg	35 KB	18/09/2001
lakeland.jpg	68 KB	18/09/2001
pmtartan.gif	79 KB	18/09/2001
lakeland.gif	155 KB	18/09/2001
pmtartan.png	321 KB	18/09/2001
gnvq3001.tif	555 KB	17/05/2003
SIP Excel.pdf	1,815 KB	05/07/2003

Name	Size	Date Modif
route.gif	15 KB	03/03/1999
consult.csv	1 KB	07/09/2001
consult.xls	16 KB	07/09/2001
agenda26.txt	1 KB	10/09/2001
project.csv	1 KB	10/09/2001
project.xls	14 KB	10/09/2001
lakeland.jpg	68 KB	18/09/2001
lakeland.gif	155 KB	18/09/2001
pmtartan.png	321 KB	18/09/2001
pmtartan.jpg	35 KB	18/09/2001
pmtartan.gif	79 KB	18/09/2001
update.txt	3 KB	18/09/2001
gnvq3001.tif	555 KB	17/05/2003
SIP Excel.pdf	1,815 KB	05/07/2003

Backing up data

For many companies their most valuable asset is their data. Computers are vulnerable to breakdown (such as a hard disk crash), earthquakes and other disasters, fire, theft and terrorism so the task of backing up must be taken seriously otherwise the data could suddenly be lost for good, which could be catastrophic.

It is essential that backup copies of the data are made frequently and since the backups could also be stolen or destroyed, a copy should regularly be stored off the site.

This applies equally to a laptop computer, which is always prone to theft. Months of work can be lost if documents, phone numbers (which can also be misused), and contact details have not been backed up.

Backup media

Floppy disks are unreliable and hold only 1.44Mb, so are generally useful only for small files.

Zip and **Jaz** drives hold up to 250Mb on a disk but are expensive.

CDs hold up to 700Mb and are cheap. **CD-R**s are write-once, so suitable for archiving data that will not change. **CD-RW**s (read/write) cost more but can be overwritten.

DVDs (**Digital Versatile Disks**) hold up to 4.7Gb which makes them very suitable.

DAT (**Digital Audio Tape**) is widely used for computer backup. Typically an organisation will have all its workstations saving their data to the file server, which backs up everything on the server to tape at night. The data is usually compressed during backup so that a typical 12Gb or 20Gb capacity cartridge will hold up to twice that amount of uncompressed data. Reading data from tape is slow but reliable.

RAID (**Redundant Array of Inexpensive Disks**) may be used by organisations who cannot afford even the briefest disruption to their data access. The data is written to two disks at once (and even another off-site) so that the operator can switch disks in case of a failure.

Internet storage is becoming popular as storage costs fall and web access speeds rise. The backup is also by definition off-site.

Methods of backup

How and how often the backup is done depends on how much data an organisation has, its importance and how often it is changed. Whatever method is used, it is important to regularly practise recovering data in case the worst happens.

Full backup is the ideal, saving all the data daily. Typically there will be a tape for each day of the week with Friday's tape being taken home. However, the backup takes several hours and ties up one machine.

In **Incremental backup** a full backup is taken one day a week, then on each subsequent day only the files created or changed on that day are backed up. This is much quicker, but if data has to be recovered the backups must be restored in the right sequence.

Some organisations, rather than deal with all their transactions immediately, keep them as **batches** to process once a day. They find it convenient to back up as a series of master files known as **Grandfather-father-son**. Here the Master File 1 for Day 1 is updated with that day's transactions to make Master File 2 for Day 2 which in turn is updated with Day 2's transactions to make Master File 3 for Day 3. The transactions are also stored so that if a master file is lost a new one can be generated.

The three tapes are rotated so that Day 3's master file is updated onto Master File 1 again on Day 4.

Viruses

Viruses are small computer programs able to replicate themselves and written with the express intention of causing annoyance or destruction. This can range from mischief – displaying joke messages and causing text characters to drop to the foot of the screen in a heap – to deleting files, using up all the memory or even reformatting the hard disk. This can cause considerable damage and downtime in a large organisation. The antidote is **antivirus** software, but since the virus writers are tirelessly changing the viruses or producing viruses that change themselves, the antivirus software must be updated at least monthly and ideally should update itself automatically online.

A virus can gain access to a computer via

❶ a floppy disk or CD

❶ a networked machine

❶ the Internet: from e-mail, web sites or downloaded files

A virus introduced on a floppy disk will 'hide' on the computer hard disk, then copy itself to any other floppy disk put in the machine by attaching itself to a file.

ORGINATION
A programmer writes a program – the virus – to cause mischief or destruction. The virus is capable of reproducing itself

TRANSMISSION
Often, the virus is attached to a normal program. It then copies itself to other software on the hard disk

REPRODUCTION
When another floppy disk is inserted into the computer's disk drive, the virus copies itself onto the floppy disk

INFECTION
Depending on what the original programmer wrote in the virus program, a virus may display messages, use up all the computer's memory, destroy data files or cause serious damage

A type of virus called a **worm** spreads itself across networks. Infected e-mail messages usually carry the virus as an attachment, usually of type **.exe**, **.vbs**, **.scr** or **.pif**. (The file may have a double extension to confuse, such as **File.txt.pif** – it is the last one that matters.) It is best not to open an attachment that you are not expecting. Some **macroviruses** exploit the **VBA (Visual Basic for Applications)** language used in Microsoft Office applications, and may infect Word, Excel or Access files. In e-mails they target the Outlook address book and mail themselves to everyone in the book, which chokes the e-mail system and makes you unpopular. Another variation generates fictitious addresses based on others it finds on your computer, and also disguises the address it comes from – making it difficult to trace. Some may pose as replies to e-mails from you, or as software upgrades 'to be installed immediately'. Yet others lure you to a fake website imitating an online bank and instruct you to confirm your log-in details – a practice known as **phishing**.

Viruses usually act at once but some lie dormant waiting to be triggered by a particular event or date – the 'Friday 13th virus being an example.

Many web sites leave a small file called a **cookie** on your machine so that they can customise the site for you the next time you visit.

Oliver Heathcote, make £27.96. Sell your past purchases at Amazon.co.uk today.

Less innocently this can also be used to implant **spyware** that sends back information such as credit card numbers, passwords and what keys have been pressed; or a **trojan horse** which makes the machine vulnerable to a later attack. You can set your browser to disable cookies but this can be inconvenient.

Logic bombs are similar to viruses and may be delivered by them. They are intended to destroy or, worse, subtly change an organisation's computer files. The 'bomb' starts work on activation from **hackers** outside the organisation who use this for extortion.

Measures to protect against viruses

Steps that reduce the risk are:

❶   Use antivirus software on every machine, running constantly and updated frequently, preferably online

❶   Check any floppy disk before putting it in a networked machine

❶   Make sure all purchased software comes in sealed, tamper-proof packaging

❶   Install **firewall** software to protect from attack over the Internet, especially with a permanently online connection

Antivirus software should be able to **disinfect** (remove the virus from) an infected file, or delete the file if it cannot.

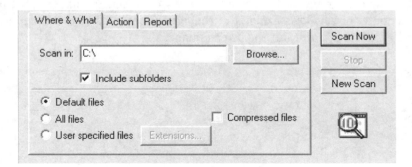

Exercise

If you have completed the exercises at the end of Chapters 2–5, you will now have a folder called **ECDLexercises** that contains several files:

Hotels.txt

Hotels.mdb

Hotels.xls

Hotels.doc

In this exercise you will practise creating, copying and moving files and folders.

1. Using **My Computer** or **Windows Explorer** locate the folder **ECDLexercises** and check that you have the files listed above.

2. Within the **ECDLexercises** folder create the subfolder structure as shown.

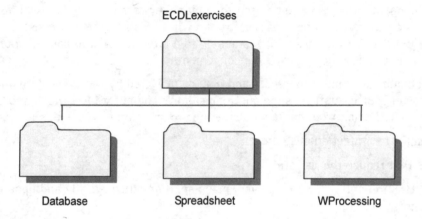

ECDLexercises

Database   Spreadsheet   WProcessing

3. Copy the file **Hotels.mdb** from **ECDLexercises** into the subfolder **Database**.

4. Delete the original copy of **Hotels.mdb** from the **ECDLexercises** folder.

5. Move the file **Hotels.xls** from **ECDLexercises** into the subfolder **Spreadsheet**.

6. Move the file **Hotels.doc** from **ECDLexercises** into the subfolder **WProcessing**

7. Rename the file **Hotels.doc** as **HotelsReport.doc**.

8. Use the **Prt Scr** key on the keyboard to capture a screen image from either **My Computer** or **Windows Explorer** of the current contents of the folder **ECDLexercises**. Print out the screen image.

Legal Issues

The collecting and holding of data about individuals as well as the misuse of computers and software has many legal implications.

Personal privacy

The **right to privacy** is a fundamental human right and one that we take for granted. Most of us, for instance, would not want our medical records freely circulated, and many people are sensitive about revealing their age, religious beliefs, family circumstances or academic qualifications. In the UK even the use of name and address files for mailshots is often felt to be an invasion of privacy.

With the advent of large computerised databases it became quite feasible for sensitive personal information to be stored without the individual's knowledge and accessed by, say, a prospective employer, credit card company or insurance company to assess somebody's suitability for employment, credit or insurance.

The Data Protection Act

The **Data Protection Act** 1998 came into force on 1 March 2000. It sets rules for processing information about people and applies to paper records as well as those held on computers. It is intended to protect the privacy of individuals.

Anyone holding personal data must comply with the eight enforceable principles of good data protection practice. They say that data must be:

- ❶ **Fairly and lawfully processed**
- ❶ **Obtained only for specific purposes** (additional data cannot be held in case it becomes useful in future)
- ❶ **Adequate, relevant and not excessive** (only the minimum amount of information required should be held)
- ❶ **Accurate** (the information must not be incorrect or misleading and must be kept up-to-date)
- ❶ **Not kept longer than necessary** (the data controller must review the personal data they hold regularly and delete any that is no longer required)

- **Processed in accordance with the data subject's rights**

- **Not transferred to other countries without adequate protection** (and specifically not outside the European Economic Area unless adequate protection is proven)

- **Secure and safe from others who don't have rights to it e.g. other employees and hackers** (The data controller should take appropriate measures to ensure that data is not accidentally or deliberately processed unlawfully or damaged)

Any organisation holding personal data about people (for example employees or customers) must register with the Data Protection Registrar. They have to state what data is being held, the sources and purposes of the data and the types of organisations to whom the data may be disclosed.

As an individual you are entitled, on making a written request to a data user, to be supplied with a copy of any personal data held about yourself. The data user may charge a fee of up to £10 for each register entry for supplying this information but in some cases it is supplied free.

Usually the request must be responded to within 40 days. If not, you are entitled to complain to the Registrar or apply to the courts for correction or deletion of the data.

Note:

There are some exemptions to the Act. These are on the grounds of national security; crime and taxation; health, education and social work; regulatory activity; journalism, literature and art; research, history and statistics; information available to the public; disclosures required by law. For more information on Data Protection and the exemptions to the act, visit www.informationcommissioner.gov.uk

Misuse and inappropriate use of computers

In the early 1980s in the UK, hacking was not illegal. Some universities stipulated that hacking, especially where damage was done to data files, was a disciplinary offence, but there was no law under which a criminal prosecution could be brought. This situation was rectified by the **Computer Misuse Act** of 1990 which defined three specific criminal offences to deal with the problems of hacking, viruses and other nuisances. The offences are:

- ❸ unauthorised access to computer programs or data
- ❸ unauthorised access with a further criminal intent
- ❸ unauthorised modification of computer material (i.e. programs or data)

To date there have been relatively few prosecutions under this law – probably because most organisations are reluctant to admit that their system security procedures have been breached, which might lead to a loss of confidence on the part of their clients.

Copyright

Computer software is **copyright** material – that means it is protected in the UK by the **Copyright, Designs and Patents Act** 1988. It is owned by the software producer and it is illegal to make or run unauthorised copies.

When you buy software it is often supplied in a sealed package (e.g. CD ROM case) on which the terms and conditions of sale are printed. This is called the software **licence** and when the user opens the package they are agreeing to abide by the licence terms. The CD or package will have a unique Product ID number which you may need to type in when installing the software. Once installed, you can see the Product ID number by clicking on the **Help** menu and selecting an option such as, for example, **About Microsoft Word**.

Software licences usually permit the user to use one copy on any single computer. It is considered to be in use if it is loaded into either the computer's temporary memory (RAM) or onto the hard disk drive. With network licences the software is often loaded onto the file server and the licence specifies how many users on the network can access it at any one time.

It is illegal to make copies of the software, except for backup purposes, so you are breaking the law if you copy some software from a friend to use on your own computer. This also includes transmitting software over a telecommunications line, thereby creating a copy

Some software is classed as **shareware**. This can be downloaded from the Internet for evaluation. If you like the program you pay a fee and register with the manufacturer. Most programs of this type allow you to use them a limited number of times and then cease to load correctly when the evaluation period expires.

Freeware programs can be downloaded from the Internet and used free.

Files downloaded from the Internet containing text, graphics, audio or video clips may also be copyright. It is illegal to use such material in your own publications without the consent of the author or creator. There has been recent publicity about the illegal downloading of music. **Peer-to-peer** networks allow computer users to exchange files with each other over the Internet. The legal status of this is controversial and this – along with freeware – is a common source of viruses, spyware and other unwanted files.

Offensive materials

Offensive materials range from abusive or racist e-mails to the downloading and storing of obscene images or data. The sending of racist abuse is no more legal as an e-mail than as a physical letter. Since many organisations keep copies of all e-mail traffic, the evidence may be around long after being deleted from the sender's computer.

The **Protection of Children Act** 1978 covers the creation, transmission, downloading, distribution and display of any offensive, obscene, indecent or menacing images, data or other material. The **Criminal Justice Act** 1988 (section 160) similarly covers the possession of these materials. Downloading material legally constitutes making a copy of it.

The persistent visiting of unsavoury web sites may not go unnoticed since **Internet Service Providers** (ISPs) in the UK have to keep records of their customers activities on the Internet.

Access controls

Most networks require a user to log on with a **user-id** and **password** before they can gain access to the computer system. The user-id is normally assigned to you, and is open to view. The password is secret and doesn't appear on the screen when you type it in – the letters may be replaced by asterisks as you type. You can change your password whenever you like.

If you are authorised to access particularly sensitive data which only certain people are allowed to view, you may need to enter a second password. For example, on a company database the Accounts clerks may be able to view customer records but not personal data about colleagues. These **access rights** are used to protect the privacy of individuals and the security of confidential data.

In order to be completely secure there are some basic rules you should follow when using a password:

❶ Never write the password down – commit it to memory

❶ Never tell your password to another person

❶ Do not use an obvious word or name as a password – a combination of at least 6 letters and numbers is best

❶ Change your password regularly

Working with Computers

People working with computers need to be protected from health and safety hazards, and the environment can also benefit from better practice in the workplace.

Ergonomics

As people spend more and more time using computers it is essential to create an **ergonomic** working environment. Ergonomics refers to design and functionality and encompasses a range of factors:

- ❶ **Lighting.** The room should be well lit. Computers should neither face windows nor back onto a window so that the users have to sit with the sun in their eyes. Adjustable blinds should be provided.

- ❶ **Ventilation.** The room should have opening windows to allow free circulation of air and to prevent overheating. This is important with laser printers, which may produce ozone when printing.

- ❶ **Furniture.** Chairs should be of adjustable height, with a backrest which tilts to support the user at work and at rest, and should swivel on a five-point base. It should be at the correct height relative to a keyboard on the desk.

- ❶ **Accessories.** Document holders, mouse mats, paper trays, foot rests etc. should be provided where appropriate.

- ❶ **Hardware.** The screen should tilt and swivel and be flicker-free. Ideally it should be situated so that it avoids reflecting light. A removable monitor filter can be useful to prevent glare. The keyboard should be separately attached.

Health and safety issues

Computers can be held responsible for many health problems, from eyestrain to wrist injuries and back.

- ❶ **Repetitive Strain Injury (RSI).** RSI is the collective name for a variety of disorders affecting the neck, shoulders and upper limbs. It can result in numbness or tingling in the arms and hands, aching and stiffness in the arms, neck and shoulders, and an inability to lift or grip objects. Using wrist and mouse supports can be helpful. The Health and Safety Executive say that more than 100,000 workers suffer from RSI.

❶ **Eyestrain**. Computer users are prone to **eyestrain** from spending long hours in front of a screen. Many computer users prefer a dim light to achieve better screen contrast, but this makes it difficult to read documents on the desk. A small spotlight focussed on the desktop can be helpful. There is no evidence that computer use causes permanent damage to the eyes, but glare, improper lighting, improperly corrected vision (through not wearing the correct prescription glasses), poor work practices and poorly designed workstations all contribute to temporary eyestrain. Larger high-resolution monitors are better. Users should be allowed regular breaks away from the computer.

❶ **Back problems**. Poor seating and bad posture whilst sitting at a computer screen can cause back problems.

❶ **Safety**. All cables should be secured and power points not overloaded. Working surfaces should be clean and tidy.

The environment

There are a number of measures that computer users can take to help the environment:

❶ Use software which puts machines into **sleep** mode after a preset period of inactivity, saving on power. Some monitors also have a sleep mode, when the screen goes blank and less power is consumed.

❶ Use screensavers to prevent a stationary image from 'burning' into the phosphor of the screen.

❶ Flat-screen monitors use less energy than **cathode ray tube (CRT)** displays.

❶ Use **Print Preview** before printing, to avoid wasting paper.

❶ Recycle printer toner cartridges.

❶ Recycle printer paper.

❶ Donate old computers to schools or charitable organisations, or send for recycling – making a new computer requires large amounts of energy and materials.

❶ CD-ROM materials, electronic documents and on-screen help all reduce the need for printed materials.

Exercises

1. Regarding the holding of personal data, which of the following principles from the Data Protection Act 1998 is true?

    A.   It can be held for ten years.
    B.   It can be freely transferred to other countries.
    C.   It must be accurate and kept up to date.
    D.   Unlimited data can be held.

2. A company may be exempt from the Data Protection Act 1998 if the data affects

    A.   Profits.
    B.   National security.
    C.   Health and safety.
    D.   Workload.

3. Which of the following is an offence under the Computer Misuse Act 1990?

    A.   Deliberately deleting important files.
    B.   Downloading adult material.
    C.   E-mailing a shareware program.
    D.   Copying customer details.

4. For a freeware program, which of the following is illegal?

    A.   Downloading it.
    B.   Making a copy of it.
    C.   E-mailing it.
    D.   Claiming it as your own.

5. A password should be:

    A.   Easy to remember.
    B.   Given to everyone.
    C.   Changed every day.
    D.   Kept private.

6. RSI is caused by:

    A.   Draughts.
    B.   Wrist strain.
    C.   Poor lighting.
    D.   Back strain.

7. Which of the following will not help the environment?

    A.   Using shorter cables.
    B.   Using screensavers.
    C.   Recycling printer toner cartridges.
    D.   Using on-screen help.